Paper Piecing

with

Alex Anderson

- Tips
- Techniques
- 6 Projects

C&T PUBLISHING

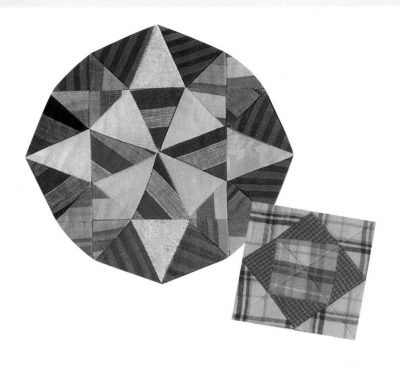

© 2002 Alex Anderson

Developmental Editor: Liz Aneloski
Technical Editor: Sara Kate MacFarland
Copy Editor: Stacy Chamness
Design Director: Diane Pedersen
Cover Designer: Christina Jarumay
Book Designer: Staci Harpole, Cubic Design
Production Assistants: Stephanie Muir and Kristy A. Konitzer
Illustrators: Jeff Carrillo and Tim Manibusan
How-To and Cover Photography: John Bagley and Richard Tauber
Cover Photo Styling: John Vitale
Quilt Photography: Sharon Risedorph
Author Photo: HGTV, 2001

Published by C&T Publishing, Inc. P.O. Box 1456, Lafayette, California 94549

Attention Teachers:
C&T Publishing, Inc. encourages you to use this book as a text for teaching. Contact us at 800-284-1114 or www.ctpub.com for more information about the C&T Teachers Program.

Library of Congress Cataloging-in-Publication Data

Anderson, Alex
  Paper piecing with Alex Anderson : tips, techniques, 6 projects.
    p. cm.
  ISBN 1-57120-138-6 (paper trade)
  1. Patchwork--Patterns. 2. Machine quilting--Patterns. I. Title.
  TT835 .A519 2002
  746.46'041--dc21

                                        2001006675

Printed in Singapore
10 9 8 7 6 5 4 3 2 1

Contents

Acknowledgements

Thank you to Karen Stone for opening up a whole new world to me, Jim Kankula for graciously sharing your expertise in paper piecing, Paula Reid and Gloria Smith for your friendship and helpful hands, P&B for awesome fabrics to work with, and C&T Publishing for your generosity and kindness in making this book possible.

Dedication

To my good friend and incredibly smart editor, Liz. This book would have been impossible without your patience and guidance. Thank you for keeping me on track!

Introduction

Because I primarily rotary cut and machine piece my quilts, *resistant* did not begin to describe my attitude when it came to paper piecing. The side blinders I had put on regarding foundation paper piecing were removed, as if by magic, the day I took Karen Stone's workshop. A whole new exciting world of quiltmaking was revealed to me. Little did I know that this time-honored style of quiltmaking would open the door of possibilities to me.

Using unusual, challenging fabrics—such as flannel, silk, and rayon—is easily manageable using paper piecing. The paper keeps the fabric stable while you are stitching pieces together.

Blocks with exposed bias edges and tiny points, which I had avoided in the past, are made easy using paper piecing. You can approach difficult patterns with the confidence that they will come out perfectly.

Delving into this interesting process of quiltmaking, I found that there are many options and opinions associated with this technique. In this book you will find what worked best for me, along with other simple options. Once you understand the basics of this great technique, you can customize your style with what works best for you.

The blocks I chose to work with are classics in the quiltmaking world. We will explore the options of working from the center out in a specific order (Square-in-a-Square and Pineapple), from one side to another in a numbered sequence (Kaleidoscope and New York Beauty), and from the center out randomly (free-form crazy patch). Each block has its own unique set of lessons to be learned.

Not all quilt blocks or patterns are appropriate for paper piecing. You must determine if a straight-line piecing sequence can be established. Blocks with Y-seams will not work. You can, however, split the Y-seam to create a straight-row sewing sequence.

Sometimes the block is constructed in paper-pieced units first, like the Kaleidoscope block, then the units are sewn together to finish the block.

You will be working with mirror images. This means that the direction of the finished block will be reversed from the pattern you see printed on the paper pattern.

The quilts are presented in order of difficulty. Square-in-a-Square is easy enough for a child to make, while the New York Beauty is a bit more challenging. The blocks are sized so that a sampler can easily be made of all the patterns. The choice is yours: Pick one quilt to make or take on the challenge of the sampler. Either way, paper piecing will broaden your approach to quiltmaking, as it has mine.

Tools and supplies

Paper for the Patterns

Computer or photocopy machine paper (20-weight) works quite nicely. It is easy to find and reasonably priced. It holds up very well when you have to pick out any sewing mistakes. However, it is difficult to see through when you are arranging the fabric in the correct position, so you will need access to good light. When it's time to pick out the paper, little fragments of paper fiber may be left in the seams. A good set of tweezers can help you get the excess fiber out. You will need to use a very short stitch and a larger sewing machine needle (80/12 or 90/14).

Typing paper is thinner and a little more transparent than computer paper. It is less durable than the computer paper but is easier to remove. Again, you will need to use a shorter stitch length and larger needle. It should go through the photocopy machine fine, but if you have problems with the photocopy machine jamming, you will need to use regular 20-weight computer/photocopy machine paper.

Velum is a high grade of tracing paper used by architects and artists. It is great to use because you can see right through it; however, it is very expensive and a bit difficult to locate. (Art stores usually carry it.) Velum is very easy to remove. Once more, you will need to use a larger needle and a shorter stitch. If you have problems with the photocopy machine jamming, you will need to use regular 20-weight computer/photocopy machine paper.

Examination paper found in a doctor's office is very lightweight and readily available if you have a generous doctor. Examination paper works great with the needle-punching technique (page 8). You can use a slightly larger stitch, and it is easy to remove.

Freezer paper (New York Beauty templates)

Freezer paper is great for making templates for piecing. Draw the shape (including seam allowances) on the dull side and cut out with paper scissors. Press (dull side up) onto the right side of the fabric and cut out. Your template can be used several times.

Rotary Cutter, Rotary Cutting Mat, and Rotary Cutting Ruler

In addition to your rotary cutter for fabric, you may also want to have a separate rotary cutter just for paper, since paper dulls blades faster than fabric. Use only mats and rulers specifically for use with rotary cutters.

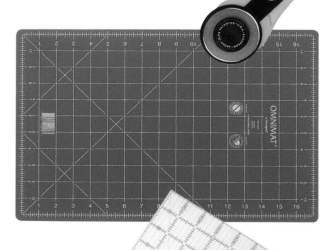

Scissors for Fabric and Paper

Just like rotary cutters, use one pair of scissors for paper and another pair for thread and fabric. This helps keep your fabric tools in excellent condition.

Pins

You have two options:
You can use heavier-weight pins that bend less as you pin the fabric onto the paper pattern, but these do not allow the paper to lie flat when aligning seams. Or, you can use lighter-weight pins that bend more easily but allow the paper to lie flatter.

Thread

You will want to use a quality cotton thread. You can either match it to the project you are working on or use a neutral gray or tan.

Extra-fine Seam Ripper

Because you will be using a smaller-than-usual stitch length, you will need a very sharp seam ripper.

Tape

Sometimes you will need to pick out seams. Because the stitch length is smaller than usual this can sometimes cause the paper to tear on the sewn line. You can use removable tape sparingly to create a temporary bond to hold the pieces together, but never use a hot iron directly on the tape—it will melt. You can also use Sewer's Fix-it Tape, which can be ironed over. If the pieces of paper are overlapped, as in the Pineapple border pattern, you can use Glue-Baste-It.

Clover MINI IRON

This is a great tool to have right next to your sewing machine for pressing each sewn seam. It uses a lot less energy than a traditional iron and gets plenty hot.

Add-A-Quarter Ruler

Use this to trim the seam allowance to an exact $1/4$" after sewing.

Surgical Tweezers

These sharp-nosed tweezers are very helpful when removing the tiny pieces of paper that can be caught in the seams after the majority of the paper is torn away.

supplies

Fabric

Paper piecing makes it possible to use specialty fabrics that quilters usually avoid working with: Silk, rayon, lamé . . . the entire range of unruly, stretchy, slippery "rebel" fabrics. However, for your first few paper-piecing projects I suggest you stick to the 100% cotton fabrics already in your stash. I have included one project made of flannels. Flannels tend to have a mind of their own but don't slip and move as much as the above-mentioned fabric "rebels."

As a self-proclaimed fabric lover I find it restricting to work with a set amount of fabric. After deciding the look of my quilt, I like to incorporate as many different fabrics as possible. It is difficult to give exact yardage amounts because there is a fair amount of waste with paper piecing. As you approach each project in this book, keep in mind that the fabric amounts listed are the *minimum* amounts you will need. I started each of the projects with several cuts of new fabric, and then I began including fabrics from my existing stash. Paper piecing is excellent for using up odd-shaped pieces of fabrics you have been saving.

Preparing the Fabric

There are two schools of thought on whether or not you should prewash your fabric when working with 100% cottons. I am of the opinion that you should. Fabric is loaded with chemicals, and I think it is best to avoid breathing and touching unwanted fabric treatments. I have found my hands chapped and my lungs congested when I have decided to pass up prewashing.

Additionally, even the best of fabrics have dyes that have been known to migrate to lighter fabrics in quilts. This is very upsetting when it happens. Many quilters have become firm believers in the importance of prewashing their fabric after this situation has occurred. As a minimum, test your fabric to see if it releases any color. You can test a fabric simply by cutting off a few square inches and boiling it in water. If it releases color, wash the fabric until the water remains clear. Re-test.

Shrinkage can also be a problem. Be especially aware of shrinkage as an issue when working with home-spun plaids or flannels.

Grain Lines

When fabric is produced, the threads are woven in two directions creating a length and a width. This is called the straight-of-grain. If you cut diagonally across the grain, you are working on the bias. Straight-of-grain has little or no stretch, while the bias can stretch to the point of disaster. In traditional piecework you should NEVER place a bias edge on the outside of a block. However, consideration of grainline is not necessary with paper piecing. The paper you are sewing the fabric onto acts as a stabilizer. It's best to avoid any outside bias edges on the blocks. However, if bias does end up on the outside edge of the block, don't worry because it will still remain true to shape. NEVER remove the paper until the entire quilt is sewn unless instructed to do so. If there is an exposed bias on the outside edge of the quilt, staystitch a little less than $1/4$" from the outside edge before removing the paper. It is best to ALWAYS have the borders on grain.

Be careful when using prints with a strong visual directional print. If they get "off" it can look strange and disorderly. Use fabrics that blend visually.

General instructions

In traditional patchwork we cut the shapes exactly the right size using a $1/4$" seam allowance on all sides. When paper piecing you should not cut the fabric pieces the exact size. It is important to cut them a little larger than anticipated. You will waste some fabric, but strange things can happen when paper piecing, and it is better to allow a little extra than to come up short.

I find it very helpful to precut shapes larger than necessary. If you are cutting strips, cut each strip *at least* $1/2$" wider and longer than the section you will cover on the pattern. If you are using half-square triangle shapes, cut the square at least 1" larger than the section you will cover on the pattern, then cut diagonally from corner to corner. For quarter-square triangles, cut the square at least $1 1/2$" larger, then cut diagonally from corner to corner, twice. In each of the projects in this book I will give you precutting sizes.

After each seam is sewn, you will trim the fabric shape leaving a $1/4$" seam allowance.

Patterns

All of the patterns in this book are meant to be photocopied. Sometimes distortion can occur when photocopying, so be sure to test the accuracy of a sample photocopy by measuring it against the original *before* making all of the necessary photocopies. Make sure that you make all of your photocopies from the same original and on the same machine.

If accuracy is a problem, or if you choose to use examination paper, consider tracing the pattern onto paper. To use the needle-punching technique, stack and staple several layers of paper together with the pattern on top. With an unthreaded sewing machine and an old needle, sew through all the layers on the drawn lines. After sewing, remove the staples. In addition to marking the lines, the paper will be easier to remove when it's time.

The patterns in this book have solid sewing lines and dashed seam allowance cutting lines. The exception is the Pineapple block pattern, where you will have to add $1/4$" seam allowance to the outside edge of the block when cutting out your patterns.

Note that the sewing order is indicated by numbers. Simply sew each piece in numerical order, trim, and press. Easy as that!

Pinning

I like to pin to assure accuracy. The pinning techniques I find useful with traditional quilting also hold true with paper piecing. The only difference is that you pin through fabric and the paper at the same time. Here are some guidelines for successful pinning.

To align seams when sewing paper-pieced units together, insert a pin no more than $1/8$" away on each side of the seam.

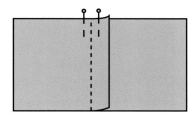

Pin $1/8$" away on each side of the seam.

When you have two components that need to align exactly (for example, the center of the Kaleidoscope block) insert the first pin from the back of one half of the block (exactly into the intersection) into the right side of the other half of the block (exactly into the intersection). Push the head of the pin firmly into both intersections. While holding the first pin tightly in place, put the second and third pins on each side of the intersection no more than $1/8$" from the first pin. Let the first pin dangle loosely. As you approach the intersection, remove the first pin at the last possible second, letting your sewing machine needle go into the same hole. I have found that this technique works very well.

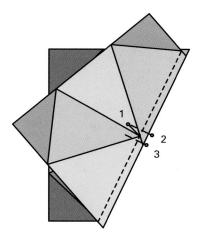

Place the second and third pins on each side of the first pin.

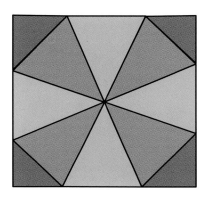

Kaleidoscope Block

If the pins end up on the underneath side, either pull out the pins as you approach them, or pin far enough away from the sewing line so your machine needle doesn't hit them and break.

Sewing Notes

Generally, you will set your machine stitch length to 18-20 stitches per inch. The stitches should be tight enough to perforate the paper for easy paper removal, but not so tight that seam ripping becomes an impossible task. Make adjustments as you see necessary. To pick out unwanted seams, cut every third or fourth stitch on one side, then gently lift the thread off of the other side.

Use an 80/12 or 90/14 universal or sharp needle. They are a little heavier, which helps penetrate both the fabric and paper, and makes paper removal easier.

When sewing, stitch two or three stitches beyond the drawn line. This allows the next line of stitches to lock the previous line of stitches in place.

For complicated patterns, or ones with long thin points, when the block is completed consider basting a few stitches on the paper tips to help hold the seam allowances in place. (Sometimes they flip in the wrong direction and get sewn into a seam.) Another option is to baste around the outside edge of the finished block. This creates one more division of paper to be removed, but it also helps prevent the seam allowances from flipping the wrong direction. You can use a large basting stitch or the regular tight stitch. The choice here is whether you prefer to remove the stitching (if you baste) or the extra section of paper to be removed (if you use a shorter stitch).

When sewing the blocks together into rows, remove the paper in the seam allowances before sewing the rows together. This allows you to press the seams in opposite directions before sewing the rows together.

DO NOT remove the remaining paper until the project instructions tell you to do so. To tear out the paper, gently run your seam ripper's long pointed tip along the seam line. It helps to weaken the paper and makes for easier removal. You can also weaken the paper by machine stitching on the lines without thread before you start paper piecing. This adds more holes in the paper and makes the paper tear more easily. Caution: If you use this technique and have to remove and re-sew a seam, there will be so many holes in the paper that it might fall apart. Quick fix: Use removable clear tape sparingly to hold the paper in place until you finish paper piecing. Be careful not to iron over it, or use Sewer's Fix-it Tape, which can be ironed over.

Pressing

I prefer ironing to finger pressing because I've seen quilters get too aggressive and stretch fabric out of shape.

Do not use steam in your iron! The water in the steam can distort and weaken the paper.

It is very important to press properly and thoroughly when paper piecing. If you are careless, tucks will be permanently pressed into the block. Many people like to "set the seams" first by simply pressing on the sewn line. This helps to lock the stitches into place. After setting the seam, flip the fabric over so that you see the right side of the fabric and press again. Make sure to avoid any tucks. The Clover MINI IRON is wonderful (page 6). Try to avoid pressing directly on the printed side of the paper. It can smudge and dirty your iron plate. I use a thin tea towel to cover the pressing surface so the ink doesn't stain my ironing board.

Planning the Quilting

Consider how you are going to quilt the top—by machine or by hand. I prefer hand quilting, since it lends a softer, homespun look. I suggest you take the time to try hand quilting. I have always enjoyed this part of the process and find that hand-quilted quilts have a special look. However, it does require a significant amount of time, and if this is a quilt that kids are going to drag around, or for a bed that the dogs jump on (I know about these things), you should try your hand at machine quilting. Your decision is determined by the look you want to achieve and/or the eventual use of the quilt.

Backing

If your quilt is 42" wide or less you will be able to use one width of fabric for your backing. This eliminates the problem of piecing the backing together. If you get carried away making blocks or want to make a larger quilt and find that your quilt top is wider than 42", you will have to sew sections of the backing fabric together to create a wide enough piece of fabric to back the whole quilt top. It's OK to use more than one cotton print for a single backing. This can be as much fun as deciding the fabric for the front of the quilt. Here are a few things to keep in mind:

1. Always prewash and cut off the selvage edges before piecing the fabric together, since it is difficult to hand quilt through the selvages and the seams won't lay flat.

2. If your quilt top has a lot of white in it, use light colors for the backing so it doesn't show through the batting to the front.

3. Always make the backing a few inches larger than the quilt top on all four sides. This is in case your quilt top shifts during quilting.

Never use a piece of decorator fabric or a sheet for the backing. They have a high thread count and are difficult to hand quilt.

Batting

For hand quilting, I recommend that you use a low-loft polyester batting. It is easier to quilt through than other batting materials.

For machine quilting, I recommend that you use 100% cotton batting. Make sure that you follow the manufacturer's instructions if it needs to be prewashed.

Layering

Depending on the size of my project, I either work on a table top (small quilt) or on my non-loop carpet (large quilt). First you must either tape down (table top) or pin using "T" pins (carpet) the backing for the quilt *wrong* side up, and work from the center of each side to the corners. Keep the fabric grain straight and get the backing stretched taut. No bubbles or ripples are acceptable, or you will have folds and tucks in the back of your finished quilt.

Tape the backing.

Carefully unroll the batting and smooth it on top of the backing. Trim the batting to the same size as the backing. Smooth the quilt top onto the batting right side up.

Basting

For Hand Quilting

Knot one end of the thread and take large stitches through all three layers.

Never baste with a colored thread, since the dye might migrate onto the fabric.

Don't bother knotting the second end of the thread to anchor your basting stitches. When it's time to remove the basting you can just give the knotted end of the thread a little tug and it will pull out.

I like to baste in a grid pattern (about every 4"), so there is an even amount of basting throughout the quilt. Never skimp on this part of the process. It will only cause disaster down the road, since your quilt layers may slip and move during the quilting process.

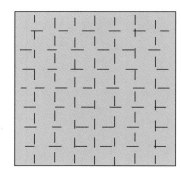

Baste in a grid.

For Machine Quilting

Unlike hand quilting, you will pin baste every 3" with safety pins. Pin evenly across the quilt, staying away from where the quilting stitches will be sewn.

Binding

Trim the batting and backing even with the edges of the quilt top. The binding holds all three layers together, and often gets the most abuse when a quilt is loved and used. There are several ways to approach bindings. I will share the simplest way with you; in the future you might want to experiment with other techniques.

1. Cut 2 $\frac{1}{4}$" x 42" strips. Trim them to the width of the quilt from side to side, plus 1" for trimming. If your quilt is over 42" wide, you will need to piece strips together to get the desired length. Create this union with a seam that is on an angle as shown. This will prevent a big lump in the binding.

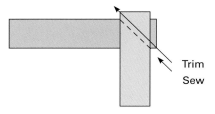

Trim
Sew

Piece the binding strips.

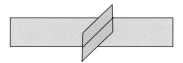

Trim the seams.

2. Fold and press lengthwise.

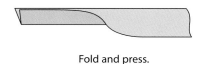

Fold and press.

3. On the top edge of the quilt, line up the raw edges of the binding with the raw edge of the quilt. Let the binding extend $1/2$" past the corners of the quilt. Sew using a $1/4$" seam allowance. Do this on the top and bottom edges of the quilt.

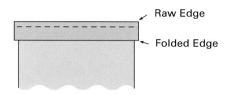

Attach the binding to the front of the quilt.

4. Flip the finished edge of the binding over the raw edge of the quilt and slip stitch the binding to the back side of the quilt. Trim the ends even with the edge of the quilt as shown.

5. Cut two $2 1/4$" x 42" strips. For the two remaining sides of the quilt, measure the length of the quilt from top to bottom. Trim the strips to this measurement plus $1/2$" for turning under. If the measurement is longer than 42", you will need to piece strips together to get the desired length. Sew the binding strips on. Fold over the ends of the binding to create a finished edge, then fold the binding to the back side. Slip stitch down.

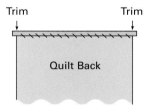

Stitch the binding and trim.

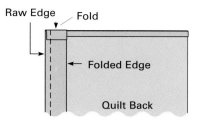

Attach the side binding.

As you travel into the world of quilting, please always keep this in mind—there isn't one definitive way to make a quilt. Each teacher has his or her own techniques and personal set of guidelines. Expose yourself to as many different approaches as possible. Take classes. Check out the local quilting guild. You will meet great people there. Soon you will become comfortable with what works for you. And remember, always sign, date, and document your project on the back side with a permanent marking pen that is designed specifically for fabric.

Square-in-a-Square Quilt

This quilt measures 50" x 56" and is made up of seventy-two 6" Square-in-a-Square blocks.
Paper pieced by Alex Anderson and machine quilted by Paula Reid.

Fabric Tips

Flannel is so much fun to work with! The number of colors and styles available is wonderful. I have collected flannels for a while and decided this was the perfect quilt for them. I separated the flannels into a light pile and a dark pile. Notice how each light block is next to a dark block and visa versa. This gives the quilt punch. Paper piecing is a good idea when you are working with fabrics that have a mind of their own. Flannel can be stretchy and unpredictable, making paper piecing a perfect choice. The paper will hold and stabilize the fabric. If you don't like "wrinkly" looking quilts, be sure to preshrink the flannel before you begin.

Fabric Requirements

The following instructions give the total amount of yardage needed to complete your quilt and are based on a 42" fabric width (page 7).

Blocks: 2 yards of light-colored flannels
Blocks: 2 yards of dark-colored flannels
Border: ¹/₂ yard
Backing: 3 ¹/₄ yards
Batting: 54" x 60"
Binding: ¹/₄ yard

Square-in-a-Square Block

Cutting

You will need 72 blocks. Make 36 A blocks that begin with a dark center and 36 B blocks that begin with a light center.

Rough Cut for Each A Block:
  Dark center square #1:
  Cut one 4" x 4" square.
  Light triangles #2 and #3:
  Cut two 3 ¹/₂" x 3 ¹/₂" squares, then cut in half diagonally.
  Dark triangles #4 and #5:
  Cut two 4 ¹/₂" x 4 ¹/₂" squares, then cut in half diagonally.

Rough Cut for Each B Block:
  Light center square #1:
  Cut one 4" x 4" square.
  Dark triangles #2 and #3:
  Cut two 3 ¹/₂" x 3 ¹/₂" squares, then cut in half diagonally.
  Light triangles #4 and #5:
  Cut two 4 ¹/₂" x 4 ¹/₂" squares, then cut in half diagonally.

Piecing

1. Cut out the paper pattern (page 18) on the dashed line.
2. Place the paper pattern *printed side down.*
3. Position the center square (#1), right side up, on the *unprinted* side of the paper pattern. If you are using a thicker paper, hold it up to the light to help position the center square.

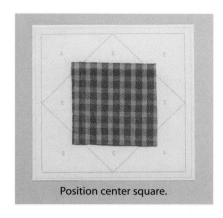

Position center square.

4. Place two light triangles (#2) on top of the center square, with right sides together, matching the raw edges. Pin.

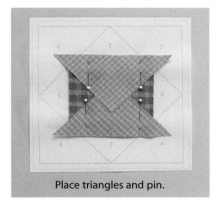

Place triangles and pin.

5. Turn the paper pattern over and stitch on both lines between 1 and 2.

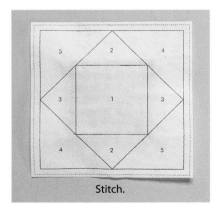

Stitch.

6. Press open.

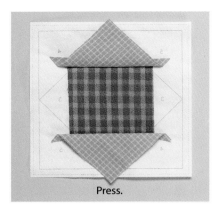

Press.

7. Place two more light triangles (#3) on opposite sides of the center square, with right sides together, matching the raw edges. Pin.

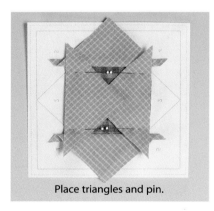

Place triangles and pin.

8. Turn the paper pattern over and stitch on both lines between 1 and 3.

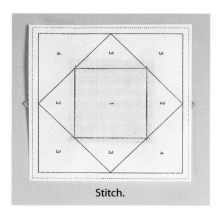

Stitch.

9. Press open.

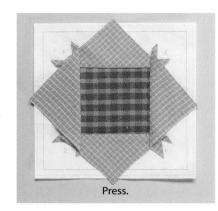

Press.

10. Fold the paper on one of the lines between 2/3 and 4.

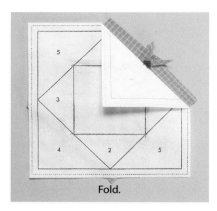

Fold.

11. Trim the seam allowance to $1/4$".

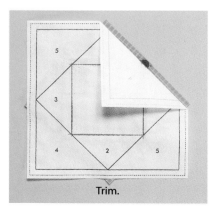

Trim.

12. Repeat Steps 10 and 11 for the three remaining edges.

Fold and trim the other three edges.

13. Place two dark triangles (#4) on opposite sides of the new square on the lines between 2/3, and 4, with right sides together, matching the raw edge with the edge that was just trimmed. Pin.

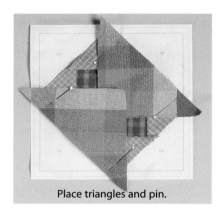

Place triangles and pin.

14. Turn the paper pattern over and stitch along the line between 2/3 and 4.

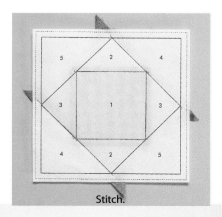

Stitch.

15. Press open.

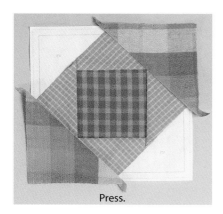

Press.

16. Place two more dark triangles (#5) on opposite sides of the square on the lines between 2/3, and 5, with right sides together, matching the raw edge with the edge that was previously trimmed and pin.

Place triangles and pin.

17. Stitch on the line.

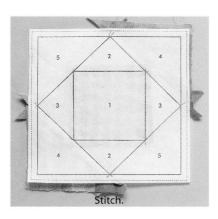

Stitch.

18. Press open.

Press.

19. Place the block with the paper on top and trim on the dashed line.

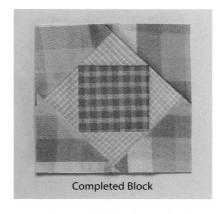

Completed Block

20. Make 36 A blocks and 36 B blocks.

Quilt Top Construction

Press following the arrows.

1. Arrange your blocks, alternating the A and B blocks, as shown, in a straight set. Make sure that every block is an alternate value colored block.
2. Sew the blocks into rows. Press following the arrows. Sew the rows together. Press.

Border

1. Cut three strips 2 $1/2$" x fabric width. Piece into one long strip and trim into two 2 $1/2$" x 54 $1/2$" strips. Sew onto the sides. Press.
2. Repeat Step 1, but trim strips 2 $1/2$" x 52 $1/2$". Sew onto the top and bottom. Press.
3. Remove the paper.

Layer, baste, quilt, and bind with guidance from the General Instructions beginning on page 8. Just in time to snuggle under on a cold winter's night!

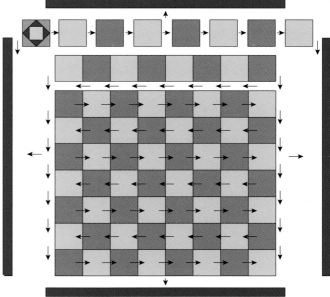

Quilt Construction

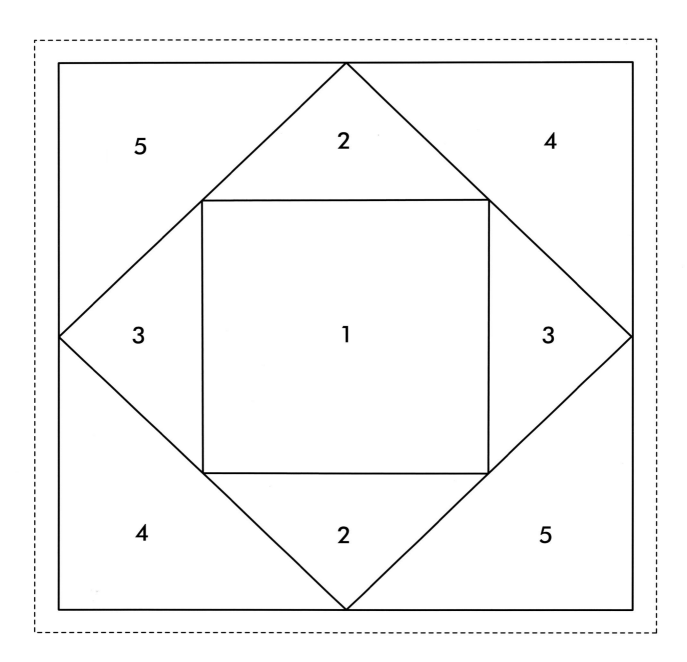

Pineapple Quilt

This quilt measures 42" x 50" and is made up of twenty 8" Pineapple blocks and eighty-four 2" x 4" Flying Geese blocks.
Paper pieced by Alex Anderson and machine quilted by Paula Reid.

Fabric Tips

Monochromatic quilts are great fun. It seemed that the color blue had taken over a lion's share of my fabric collection, so it was time to get busy and use up some of it. I love mixing and matching fabrics collected over the years. Notice that both beige and white were used as the neutrals. By using previously collected fabrics with new acquisitions, it gives me permission to collect more! The Flying Geese block is an excellent candidate to paper piece because of the exposed bias edges. The paper keeps the edges from stretching out of shape.

Fabric Requirements

The following instructions give the total amount of yardage needed to complete your quilt and are based on a 42" fabric width (page 7).

Blocks and border: 4 $^1/_2$ yards of blue (dark)

Blocks and border: 4 yards of neutrals (light)

Inner border: $^1/_4$ yard

Backing: 1 $^1/_2$ yards (if the backing is 44" wide—if not, double the amount)

Batting: 46" x 54"

Binding: $^1/_2$ yard

Pineapple Block

Cutting

You will need 20 Pineapple blocks.

Rough Cut: (for each block)
Center Square: Cut one 1 $^3/_4$" x 1 $^3/_4$" square.
Strips: Cut one 1 $^1/_2$" strip of each fabric.
Corners: Cut two 3 $^1/_2$" x 3 $^1/_2$" squares, then cut in half diagonally.

Piecing

The odd numbers will be light strips, and the even numbers and corners will be dark strips.

1. Cut out the paper pattern (page 26) $^1/_4$" beyond the solid line.

2. Place the paper pattern *printed side down.*

3. Position the center square, right side up, on the *unprinted* side of the paper pattern. If you are using a thicker paper, hold it up to the light to help position the center square.

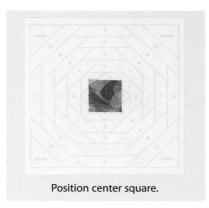

Position center square.

4. Place a light strip (#1) on top of the center square, with right sides together, matching the raw edges. Trim the strip to the approximate length of the piece you are aligning it to. Pin.

Place a strip and pin.

5. Turn the paper pattern over and stitch on the line between 1 and 2.

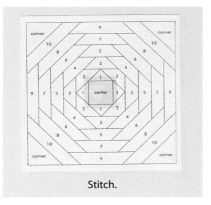

Stitch.

6. Press open.

Press.

7. Repeat Steps 4-6 to add the opposite #1 strip.

Place, pin, stitch, and press.

8. Repeat Steps 4-6 to add the two remaining #1 strips.

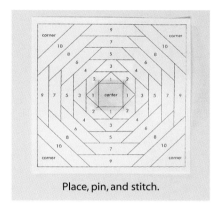

Place, pin, and stitch.

Press.

9. Fold the paper on one of the lines between 1 and 2.

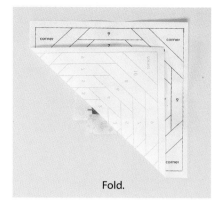

Fold.

10. Trim the seam allowance to $1/4$".

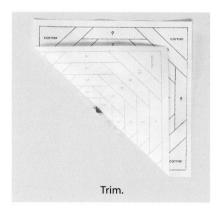

Trim.

11. Repeat Steps 9 and 10 to trim the three remaining edges.

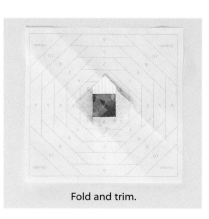

Fold and trim.

12. Place a dark strip (#2) on top of the #1 triangles, with right sides together, matching the raw edges. Trim the strip to the approximate length of the piece you are aligning it to. Pin.

Place a strip and pin.

13. Turn the paper pattern over and stitch on the line between 1 and 2.

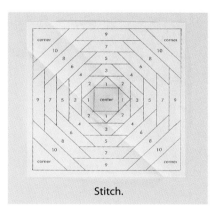

Stitch.

14. Press open.

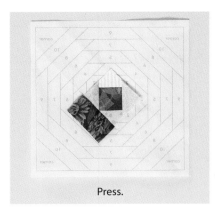

Press.

15. Repeat Steps 12-14 to add the opposite #2 strip.

Place, pin, stitch, and press.

16. Repeat Steps 12-14 to add the two remaining #2 strips.

Place, pin, stitch, and press.

17. Fold the paper on one of the lines between 2 and 3.

18. Trim the seam allowance to ¼".

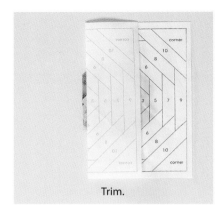

Trim.

19. Repeat Steps 17 and 18 for the three remaining edges.

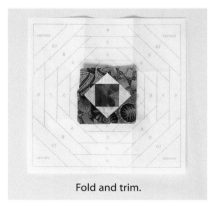

Fold and trim.

20. Repeat, adding four light strips (on the odd numbers), then four dark strips (on the even numbers) until you have covered the paper pattern.

Untrimmed Block

21. Place the block with the paper on top and trim ¼" past the solid outer line to leave ¼" seam allowance. You may be cutting beyond the paper pattern.

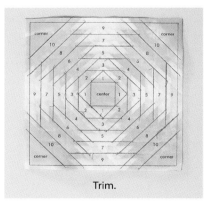

Trim.

Completed Block

Flying Geese Border

Cutting

You will need a total of 84 Flying Geese.

Rough Cut (for each unit):
    Triangles for #1: Cut one 5 1/2" x 5 1/2" square, then cut in half diagonally twice.
    Triangles for #2 and #3: Cut one 3 1/2" x 3 1/2" square, then cut in half diagonally.

Piecing

1. Make 22 photocopies of the Flying Geese Border pattern (5 for the top, 5 for the bottom, and 6 for each side border). Cut out the paper patterns on the dashed lines. Tape the paper patterns together for each border, matching the lines, using a product that can be ironed (such as Glue-Baste-It! or Sewer's Fix-it Tape). Be sure there is 1/4" seam allowance on all sides. (Add the dashed line if necessary.) You will need two paper patterns that have 21 Flying Geese (for the side borders), two paper patterns that have 19 Flying Geese (for the top and bottom borders), and two paper patterns that have 2 Flying Geese (also for the top and bottom borders).

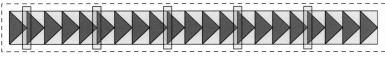

Taped Side Border Pattern

 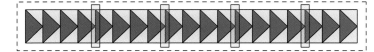

Taped Top and Bottom Border Pattern

2. Place the paper pattern *printed side down*. Position the center triangle (#1) on the *unprinted* side of the paper pattern. If you are using a thicker paper, hold it up to the light to help position the center triangle.

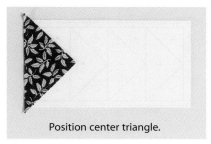

Position center triangle.

3. Place the next triangle (#2) on top of the center triangle with right sides together, matching the raw edges, and pin.

Place triangle on top and pin.

4. Turn the paper pattern over and stitch on the line between 1 and 2.

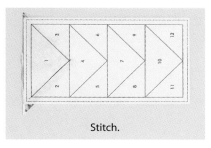

Stitch.

5. Press open.

Press.

6. Place the next triangle (#3) on top of the center triangle with right sides together, matching the raw edges and pin.

Place triangle on top and pin.

7. Turn the paper pattern over and stitch on the line between 1 and 3. Press open.

Stitch and press.

8. Fold the paper on line 2/3 and 4. Trim leaving ¼" seam allowance.

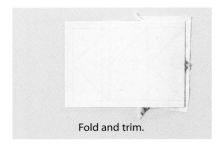

Fold and trim.

9. Place triangle #4 on the trimmed edge. Pin, sew, and press.

Pin, sew, and press.

10. Repeat Steps 3-9 to add pieces to complete the border section.

11. Trim on the dashed line. Repeat to paper piece all border sections.

Quilt Top Construction

Press following the arrows.

1. Arrange your blocks as shown in a straight set.

2. Sew the blocks in rows. Press following the arrows. Sew the rows together. Press.

Inner Border

1. Cut two strips 1 ½" x 40 ½". Sew onto the sides. Press toward the inner border.

2. Cut two strips 1 ½" x 34 ½". Sew onto the top and bottom. Press toward the inner border.

3. Remove the paper on the quilt top either now or after the final border has been sewn on.

Outer Border

1. Attach the side borders. Press.

2. Refer to the illustration for the correct placement and attach a border corner section to the left end of the top border section.

3. Attach this border to the top edge of the quilt. Press.

4. Refer to the illustration for the correct placement and attach a border corner section to the right end of the bottom border section.

5. Attach this border to the bottom edge of the quilt. Press.

6. Carefully remove the paper.

Your efforts were well worth it! Now it's time to layer, baste, and quilt following the General Instructions beginning on page 8.

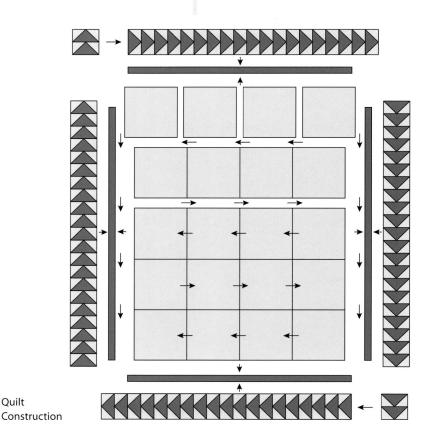

Quilt Construction

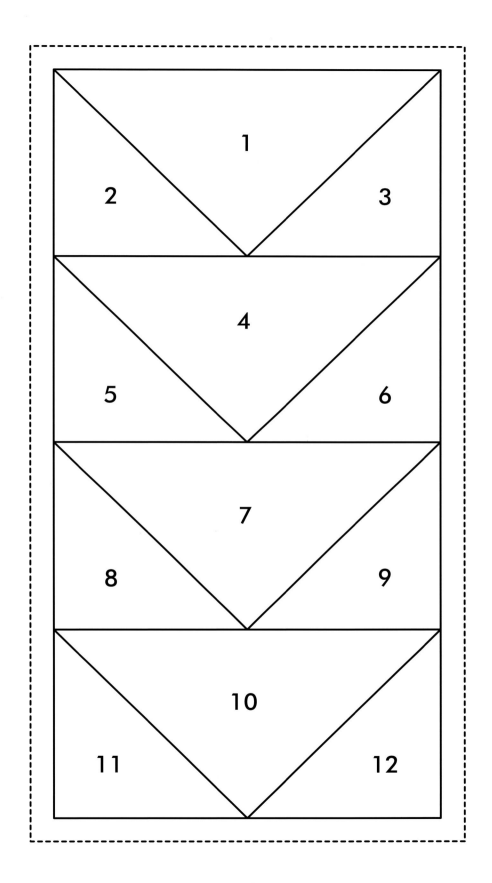

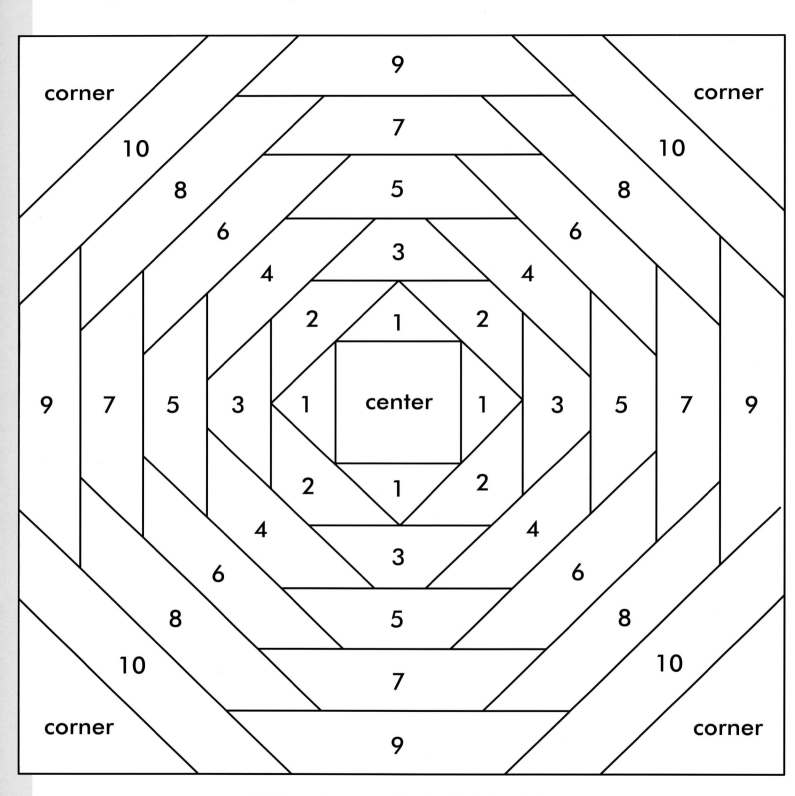

Add ¼" seam allowance to outside edge of block when trimming.

Kaleidoscope Quilt

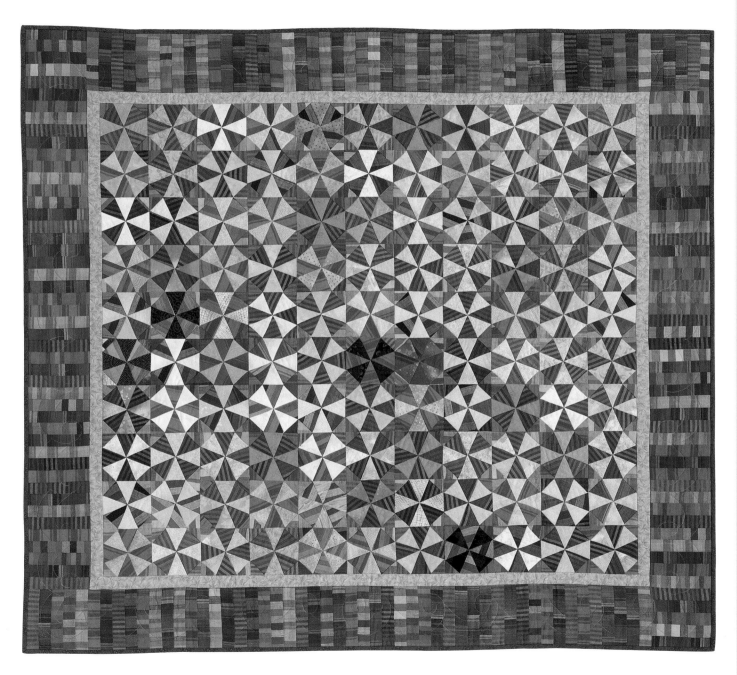

This quilt measures 52" x 56" and is made up of one hundred ten 4" Kaleidoscope blocks.
Paper pieced by Alex Anderson and machine quilted by Paula Reid.

Fabric Tips

This quilt was inspired by Kaffe Fassett's entire striped collection. The colors were a delight to my eye. To add contrast I worked mostly with pastels to complement the stripes. In order to get the circular motion, half the blocks are value colored one way, the other half the other way.

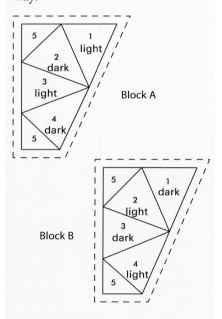

Fabric Requirements

The following instructions give the total amount of yardage needed to complete your quilt and are based on a 42" fabric width (page 7).

Blocks: 4 1/2 yards of stripes (3 1/4 yards of darks and 1 1/4 yards of mediums)

Blocks: 3 1/4 yards of light-colored fabrics

Inner border: 1/4 yard

Outer border: 1 1/4 yards

Backing: 3 1/2 yards

Batting: 56" x 60"

Binding: 1/3 yard

Kaleidoscope Block

Cutting

You will need 110 blocks. Make 55 A blocks and 55 B blocks.

Rough Cut for Each A and B Block:

Triangles for #1-4: Cut two light rectangles 4" x 5", then cut in half diagonally. Cut two dark rectangles 4" x 5", then cut in half diagonally.

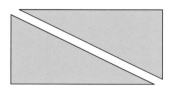

Cut in half diagonally.

Triangles for #5: Cut two medium-colored squares 2 1/2" x 2 1/2", then cut in half diagonally.

Piecing for Block A

1. Cut out the paper pattern on the dashed line.

2. Stack one light (#1) and one dark A triangle (#2) with right sides together and the light triangle on top.

3. Place the paper pattern, *printed side up*, on top of the fabric triangles. Be sure the edges of the fabric extend at least 1/4" past the lines on the paper pattern. Pin.

4. Stitch along the line between 1 and 2.

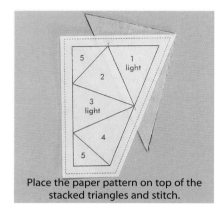

Place the paper pattern on top of the stacked triangles and stitch.

5. Fold the paper on the stitched line and trim the seam allowance to 1/4".

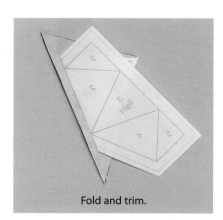

Fold and trim.

6. Press open.

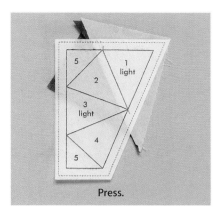

Press.

7. Fold the paper on the line between 2 and 3.

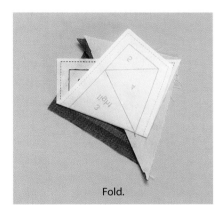

Fold.

8. Trim the seam allowance to ¼".

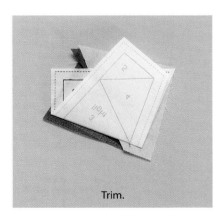

Trim.

9. Turn the paper pattern over and place a light A triangle (#3) on top of the dark triangle, right sides together, matching the raw edge of the longest side with the edge that was just trimmed. Pin.

Place a light A triangle and pin.

10. Turn the paper pattern over and stitch along the stitching line between 2 and 3.

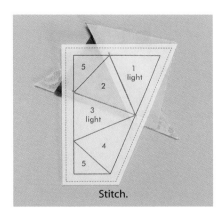

Stitch.

11. Press open.

Press.

12. Fold on the line between 3 and 4 and trim the seam allowance to ¼".

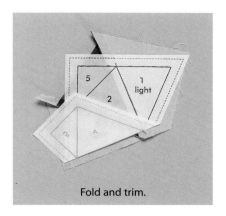

Fold and trim.

13. Turn the paper pattern over and place a dark A triangle (#4) on top of the light triangle, with right sides together, matching the raw edge of the longest side with the edge that was just trimmed. Pin.

Place a dark B triangle and pin.

14. Turn the paper pattern over and stitch along the line between 3 and 4.

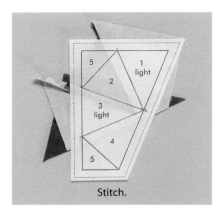

Stitch.

15. Press open.

Press.

16. Fold the paper on the lines between 2 and 5, and between 4 and 5. You may have to tear the paper pattern slightly to fold on the lines.

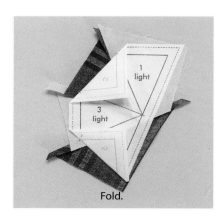

Fold.

17. Trim the seam allowances to ¼".

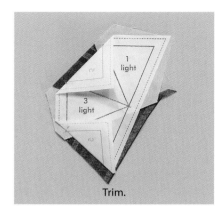

Trim.

18. Turn the paper pattern over and place two medium-colored B triangles as shown, with right sides together, matching the raw edges with the edges that were just trimmed. Pin.

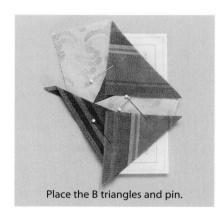

Place the B triangles and pin.

19. Stitch on the line.

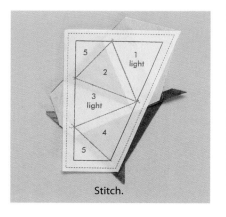

Stitch.

20. Press open.

Press.

21. Place the pieced section *with the paper on top*, and trim on the dashed line.

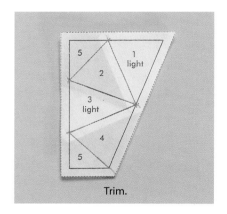

Trim.

Completed half of block

22. Repeat to make the second half of the block.

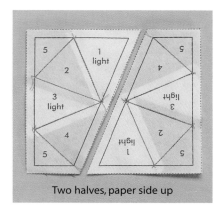
Two halves, paper side up

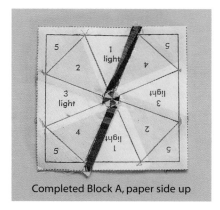
Completed Block A, paper side up

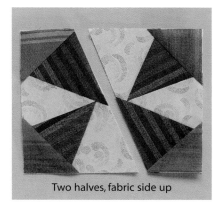
Two halves, fabric side up

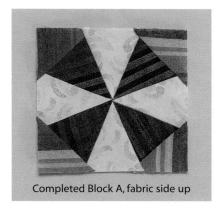
Completed Block A, fabric side up

23. Place the two halves with right sides together. Pin (page 9).

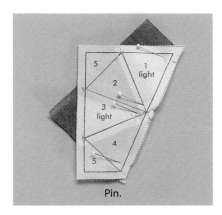
Pin.

24. Stitch on the sewing line. Remove the paper from the seam allowance. Press as shown.

25. Trim to ¹/₄" around the outside edge.

26. Make 55 A Blocks.

27. Make 55 B Blocks following the instructions above, but use the Block B pattern and fabrics. Notice that the lights and darks are reversed.

Quilt Top Construction

Press following the arrows.

1. Arrange your blocks as shown on page 32 in a straight set. Alternate Block A, Block B, and so on for the first row; Block B, Block A, and so on for the second row. Continue alternating the blocks for all rows. This alternating arrangement forms the circles in the pattern design.

2. Sew the blocks into rows. Press following the arrows. Sew the rows together. Press.

Inner Border

1. Cut two strips 1 ¹/₂" x 40 ¹/₂". Sew onto the top and bottom. Press toward the inner border.

2. Cut two strips at 1 ¹/₂" x 42". Sew onto the sides. Press toward the inner border.

3. Remove the paper now, or after the final border has been sewn on.

Outer Border

1. Cut 204 rectangles 1 ¹/₂" x 5 ¹/₂".

2. Stitch 46 rectangles together to make one side border. Repeat to make the second side border.

3. Attach the side borders. Press.

4. Stitch 47 rectangles together to make a top border section. Repeat to make a bottom border section. Stitch 5 rectangles together to make a border corner section. Repeat to make a second border corner section.

5. Refer to the illustration on page 32 for the correct placement and attach a border corner section to the left end of the top border section.

6. Attach this border to the top edge of the quilt. Press.

7. Refer to the illustration for the correct placement and attach a border corner section to the right end of the bottom border section.

8. Attach this border to the bottom edge of the quilt. Press.

9. Remove the paper if you haven't already.

Congratulations, your Kaleidoscope quilt is completed! Now it's time to layer, baste, and quilt, with guidance from the General Instructions beginning on page 8.

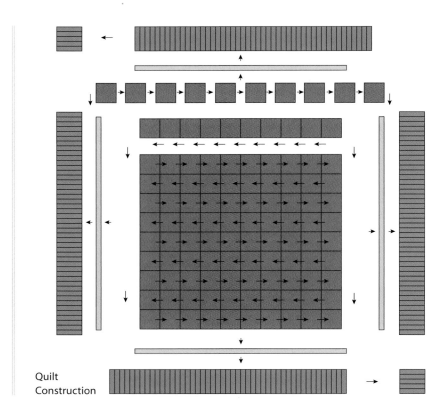

Quilt Construction

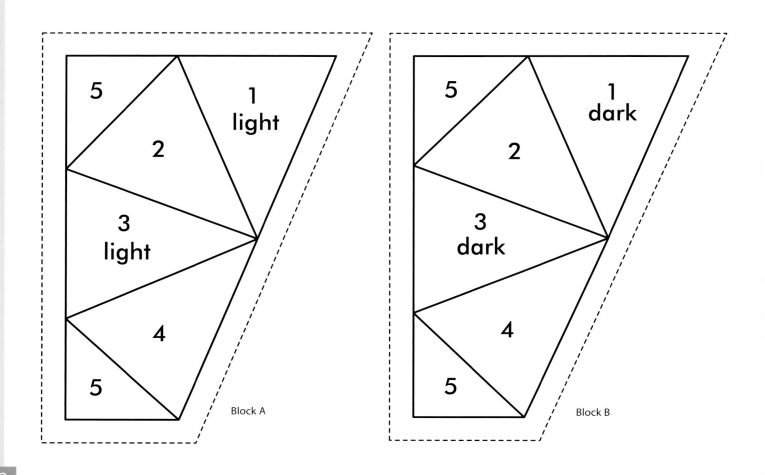

Block A

Block B

New York Beauty Quilt

This quilt measures 39" x 39" and is made up of sixteen 8" New York Beauty blocks and a 3½"-wide spiked border.
Paper pieced and machine quilted by Gloria Smith.

Fabric Tips

The delight and excitement of my first fabric line, Color Bridge by P&B Textiles, was beyond words. To see quilts made entirely from my collection was a pleasure I had not anticipated. My friend Gloria Smith stepped up to the machine and worked with the fabrics expertly. Thanks Gloria, your work is awesome! (Gloria recommends that you make a couple of practice blocks.)

Fabric Requirements

The following instructions give the total amount of yardage needed to complete your quilt and are based on a 42" fabric width (page 7).

Purples: $1/2$ yard for spikes
Blues and teals: $1 2/3$ yards
  for spikes
Reds and pinks: $1 2/3$ yards
  for spikes
Orange: $1/3$ yard for the
  inner arcs
Yellow: $1/2$ yard for the centers
Yellow: $2 1/2$ yards for the
  background
Backing: $1 1/4$ yards
Batting: 43" x 43"
Binding: $1/3$ yard

New York Beauty Block

Cutting

You will need 16 blocks.

Rough Cut: (for each block)
  Background: Cut one 3" strip.
  Spikes: Cut one $2 1/2$" x $4 1/2$" rectangle from each fabric.

Piecing

1. Cut out the arc pattern (page 39) on the dashed line.

2. Place a background strip (#1) and a spike rectangle (#2), right sides together, with the strip on top.

3. Place the paper pattern, *printed side up*, on top of the fabric. Be sure the edges of the fabric extend at least $1/4$" past the lines on the paper pattern. Pin.

4. Stitch along the stitching line between 1 and 2.

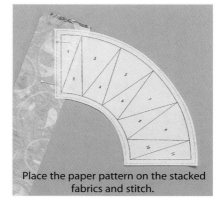

Place the paper pattern on the stacked fabrics and stitch.

5. Turn the paper pattern over and fold on the stitched line and trim the seam allowance to $1/4$".

6. Press open.

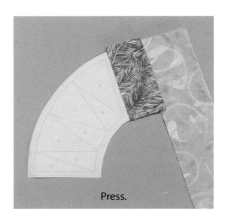

Press.

7. Turn the paper pattern over and fold the paper on the line between 2 and 3.

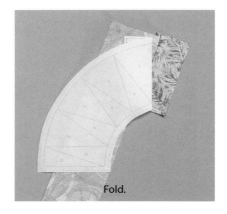

Fold.

8. Trim the seam allowance to $1/4$".

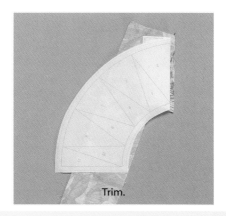

Trim.

9. Trim off the extra background strip length.

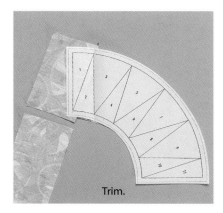

Trim.

10. Turn the paper pattern over and place a background strip (#3) on top of the spike fabric, with right sides together, matching the raw edge with the edge that was just trimmed. Pin.

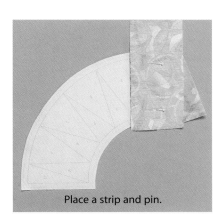

Place a strip and pin.

11. Turn the paper pattern over and stitch along the stitching line between 2 and 3.

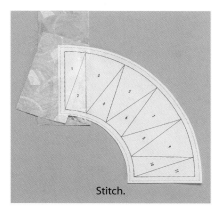

Stitch.

12. Turn the paper pattern over and press open.

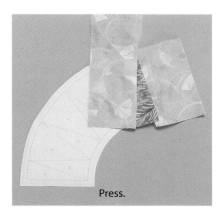

Press.

13. Turn the paper pattern over and fold the paper on the line between 3 and 4, and trim the seam allowance to $1/4$". Trim off the excess strip.

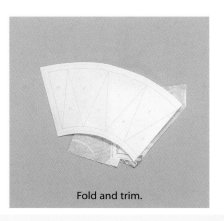

Fold and trim.

14. Turn the paper pattern over and place a spike rectangle (#4) on top of the background piece, with right sides together, matching the raw edge with the edge that was just trimmed. Pin.

Pin.

15. Turn the paper pattern over and stitch along the line between 3 and 4.

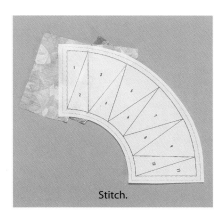

Stitch.

16. Repeat from Step 6, adding background strips and spike rectangles to complete the arc.

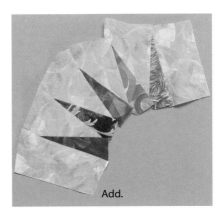
Add.

17. Place the pieced arc *with the paper pattern on top*, and trim on the dashed line.

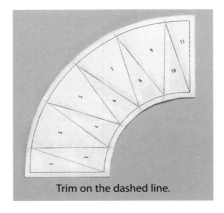
Trim on the dashed line.

Block Construction

1. Trace patterns A, B, and C (pages 39-40) onto the dull side of the freezer paper and cut out on the dashed line. Press A onto the background fabric, B onto inner arc fabric, and C onto center fabric.

2. Cut out A, B, and C on the dashed line. Your freezer paper template can be used up to six times.

Block pieces laid out.

3. Fold A in half and finger press to mark the center of the curved edge.

4. Match the center of the pieced arc and the center of the curved edge of A and pin. Then pin the two outside edges. Pin slightly away from the curved edge.

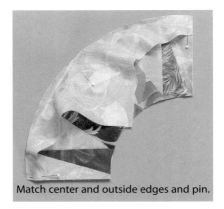
Match center and outside edges and pin.

5. Continue pinning the curve, aligning the raw edges.

Continue pinning.

6. Turn the paper pattern over and stitch along the solid ¹/₄" sewing line. Press toward A.

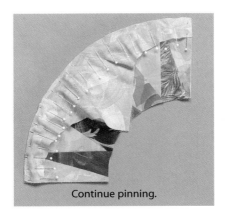
Stitch and press.

7. Remove the paper from the pieced arc.

8. Fold B in half and finger press to mark the center of the longer curved edge.

9. Match the center of the pieced arc with the center of B and pin. Then pin the two outside edges as you did in Step 4.

Smaller arcs are a little trickier to maneuver than larger arcs. Clip the seam allowance of the convex curve ($^1/_8$" deep) to help ease the curve into position.

10. Continue pinning the curve, aligning the raw edges.

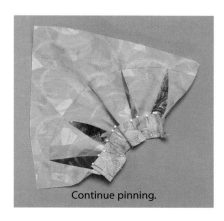
Continue pinning.

11. Stitch using $^1/_4$" seam allowance with B on top. Press toward B.

Press.

12. Repeat Steps 8-11 to add piece C. Stitch with C on top. Press toward B.

Completed Block

Quilt Top Construction

Press following the arrows.

1. Arrange your blocks as shown on page 38 in a straight set.

2. Sew the blocks into rows. Press.

3. Sew the rows together. Press.

Borders

Paper piece 16 of the $3^1/_2$" x 8" spiked border units using the same procedure as the arcs. Sew four units together to create one border. Make a total of four borders (one for each edge of the quilt). You will paper piece these as you did the arcs. Do NOT remove the paper yet.

Border Corners
1. Trace C and D onto the dull side of the freezer paper and cut out on the dashed line. Press C onto the background fabric and D onto inner arc fabric.

2. Cut out C and D on the dashed line. Remove the freezer paper. Your freezer paper template can probably be used for all four corners.

Block pieces laid out.

3. Fold C in half and finger press to mark the center of the curved edge.

4. Match the center of the arc and the center of the curved edge of C and pin. Then pin the two outside edges. Continue pinning the curve, aligning the raw edges.

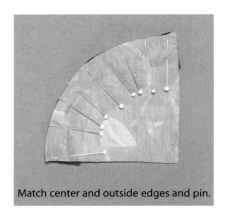

Match center and outside edges and pin.

5. Sew and press toward D.

Stitch.

Attaching the Borders

1. Sew the top and bottom borders onto the quilt. Press toward the quilt top.

2. Sew the corners onto the two side borders.

3. Sew the side borders on and press toward the quilt top.

4. Carefully remove the paper.

Congratulations! Not only have you mastered spikes, but pieced curves, too! Now it is time to layer, baste, and quilt following the General Instructions beginning on page 8.

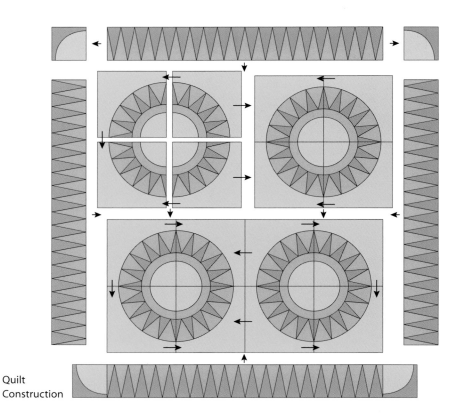

Quilt Construction

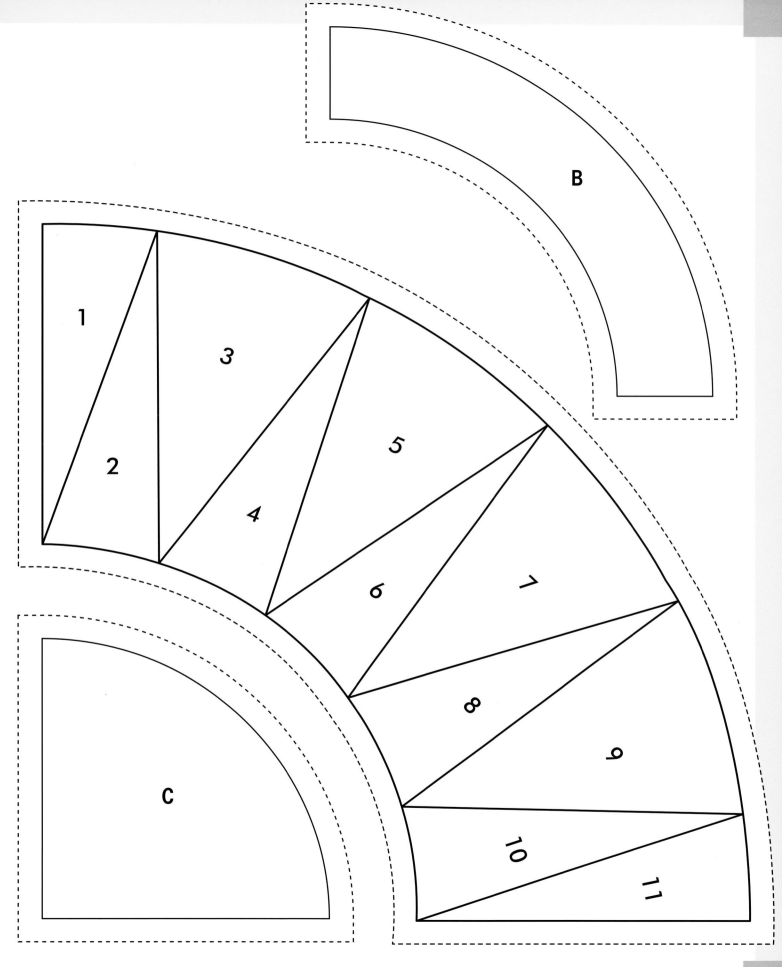

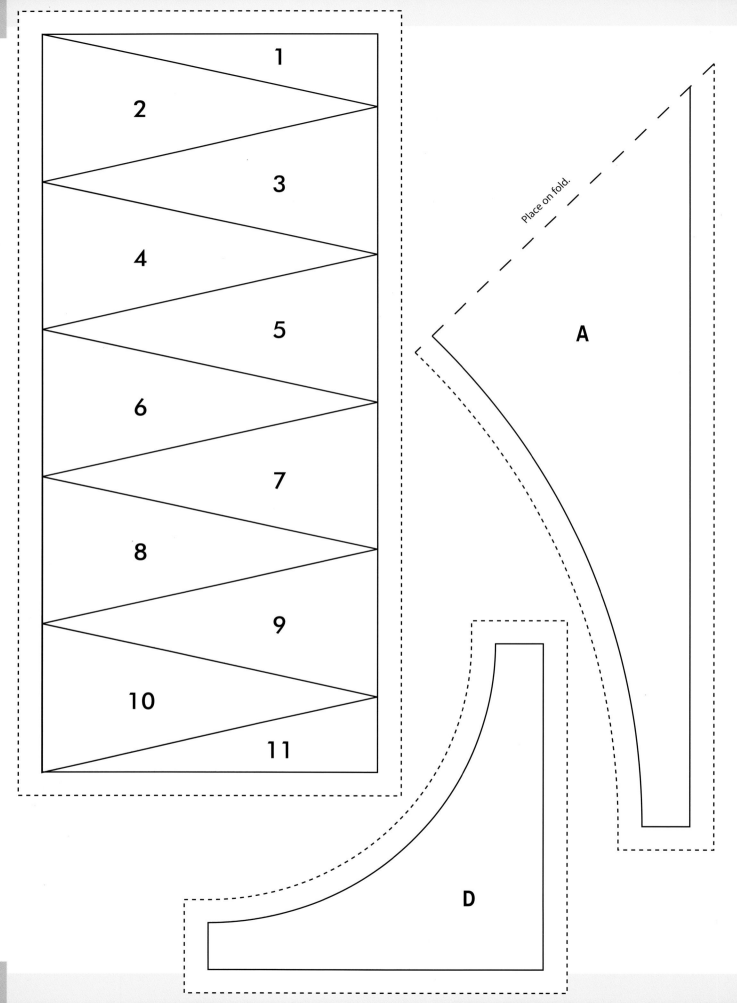

1

2

3

4

5

6

7

8

9

10

11

Place on fold.

A

D

Basket Quilt
with Paper-Pieced Crazy-Patch Center

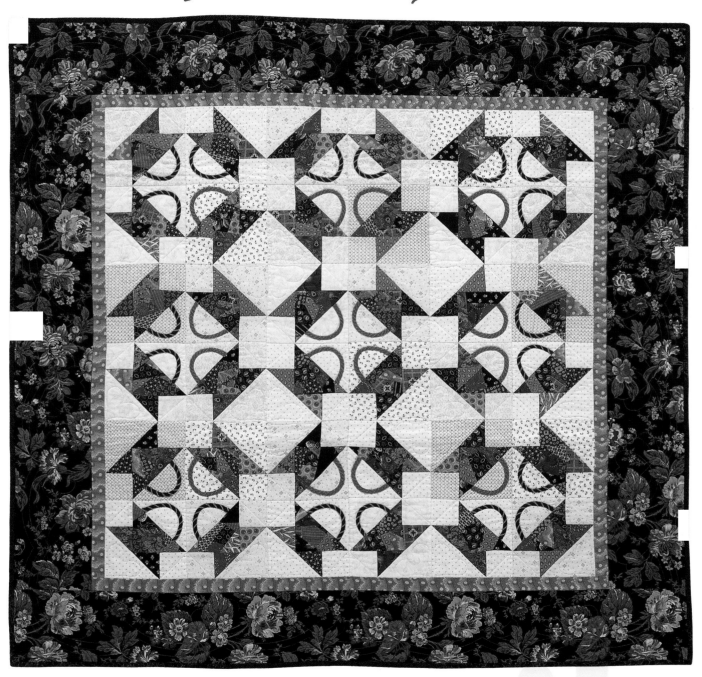

This quilt measures 49" x 49" and is made up of thirty-six 6" Crazy-Patch Basket blocks.
The crazy-patch section of the basket is paper pieced and the rest of the block is traditionally pieced.
Paper pieced by Alex Anderson and machine quilted by Paula Reid.

Fabric Tips

When I saw this border fabric, crazy-patch baskets began dancing before my eyes. It not only had a rich deep brown coloration, but hints of blue and green also graced the surface. To keep the vintage look, I used primarily reproduction fabrics from all four color families represented in the border fabric. Notice how two colors were used for the handles, both in stripes. Several different background fabrics were used to continue the scrappy look often found in older quilts. This project is perfect for a scrap bag of odd-shaped fabrics.

Fabric Requirements

The following instructions give the total amount of yardage needed to complete your quilt and are based on a 42" fabric width (page 7).

Baskets: 3 1/2 yards of medium to dark scraps
Handles: 1/3 yard of medium to dark scraps
Background: 1 1/2 yards of light-colored fabrics
Inner border 1/4 yard
Outer border: 1 1/3 yards
Backing: 3 1/4 yards
Batting: 53" x 53"
Binding: 3/8 yard

Crazy-Patch Basket Block

Cutting

You will need 36 blocks.

Piecing

Use a 1/4" seam allowance.

Each crazy-patch section is unique to itself. The trick is to create straight lines to sew each new patch to. Use small scraps.

1. Cut out the basket paper pattern (page 44) 1/2" beyond the dashed line.
2. Cut an irregular three- or five-sided patch about 2" in size.
3. Center and pin the shape, right side up, to the *unprinted* side of the paper.

Pin center onto pattern.

4. Select a piece of fabric that is at least as long as one of the sides. Pin in place and stitch using 1/4" seam allowance.

Pin in place.

5. Press open.

Press.

6. Trim the fabric to create a straight edge to align the next piece of fabric.

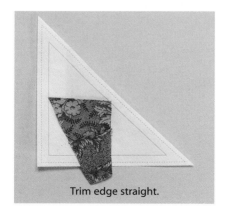
Trim edge straight.

7. Select another piece of fabric and align it to another edge. Pin and stitch.

Pin and stitch.

8. Press open.

Press.

9. Continue until the entire triangle is covered with fabric. Remember to trim the fabric to create a straight edge to align the next piece of fabric.

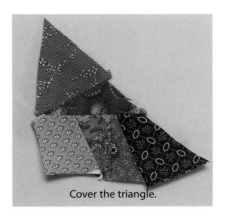
Cover the triangle.

10. Trim the fabric on the dashed line.

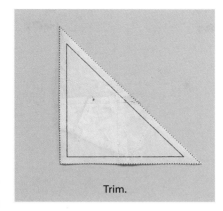
Trim.

Block Construction

1. Cut one square $2^{7}/_{8}$", then cut in half diagonally for the basket.

2. Cut one square $4^{7}/_{8}$", then cut in half diagonally for the background. Staystitch $^{1}/_{8}$" from the raw edge on the background piece that the handle will be sewn onto.

3. Cut two $2^{1}/_{2}$" squares for the background.

4. Cut a bias strip 1" x $6^{1}/_{2}$" for the basket handle. Press in half lengthwise. Staystitch $^{1}/_{8}$" in from the long raw edges.

Staystitch, draw the handle, press bias lengthwise.

5. Trace a handle placement line with a removable marking tool, referring to the photo for handle placement. (Always test your marker on a scrap of fabric to make sure it is removable from your fabric.)

6. Pin the handle to the background fabric with the raw edges facing out.

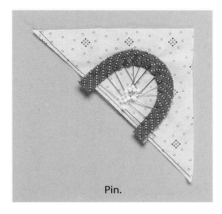
Pin.

7. Stitch a scant $^{1}/_{4}$" from the raw edge of the handle. Press the finished edge over the raw edge. Appliqué the finished edge of the handle.

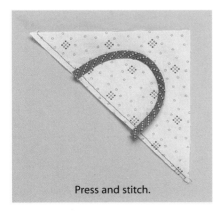
Press and stitch.

8. Stitch the basket handle/background triangle to the crazy-patch block. Press toward the handle section. Join the small triangle and the square lining up the straight edges on both sides.

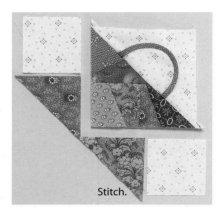

Stitch.

9. Sew the triangle/square units to the base. Sew on the bottom triangle and press toward the bottom triangle. Remove the paper.

Stitch.

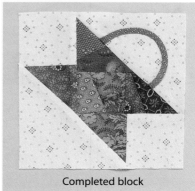

Completed block

Quilt Top Construction

Press following the arrows.

1. Arrange your blocks as shown in a straight set.
2. Sew the blocks in rows. Press following the arrows. Sew the rows together. Press.

Inner Border

1. Cut two strips $1\,^1/_2$" x $36\,^1/_2$". Sew onto the top and bottom. Press toward the inner border.
2. Cut two strips $1\,^1/_2$" x $38\,^1/_2$". Sew onto the sides. Press toward the inner border.

Outer Border

1. Cut two strips 6" x $38\,^1/_2$". Sew onto the top and bottom. Press toward the outer border.
2. Cut two strips 6" x $48\,^1/_2$". Sew onto each side. Press toward the outer border.

Congratulations, your quilt top is completed! Now it's time to layer, baste, and quilt following the General Instructions beginning on page 8.

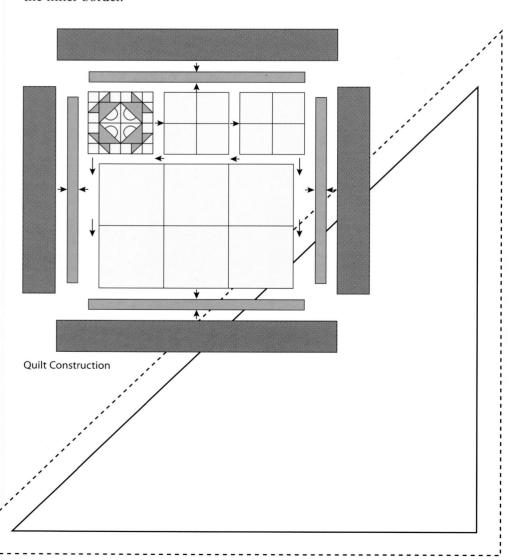

Quilt Construction

sampler Quilt

*This quilt measures 40½" x 40½" and contains six 6" Square-in-a-Square, four 6" Kaleidoscope,
four 6" Basket, four 12" New York Beauty, and two 12" Pineapple blocks.
Pieced by Alex Anderson and machine quilted by Paula Reid.*

Fabric Tips

I don't usually work with specific fabric collections, but this group of fabrics by Piece of Cake (P&B Textiles) really caught my eye. The playfulness looked perfect for a sampler. The challenge was how to mix and match them. I discovered that the key was to separate them by value to give order to this fun group of fabrics.

To complete the quilt pictured you will need to make:

Six 6" (finished) Square-in-a-
   Square blocks
Four 6" (finished) Kaleidoscope
   blocks
Four 6" (finished) Basket blocks
Four 12" (finished) New York
   Beauty blocks
Two 12" (finished) Pineapple
   blocks

Fabric Requirements

Fabric requirements are based on 42" fabric width (page 7).

Light-colored fabrics: 1 yard
   total of a variety of fabrics
Medium-colored fabrics: 1/2 yard
   total of a variety of fabrics
Dark-colored fabrics: 1 yard
   total of a variety of fabrics
Inner border: 1/4 yard stripe
Backing: 1 1/4 yards
Batting: 45" x 45"
Binding: 1/4 yard

Sampler

Cutting and Piecing

SQUARE-IN-A-SQUARE BLOCK

Refer to pages 15-17 and 18 for guidance. Make 3 A blocks and 3 B blocks.

PINEAPPLE BLOCK

Refer to pages 20-22 and 26 for guidance. Make 2 blocks.

KALEIDOSCOPE BLOCK

Refer to pages 28-31 and 32 for guidance. Make 2 A blocks and 2 B blocks.

NEW YORK BEAUTY BLOCK

Refer to pages 34-37 and 39-40 for guidance. Make 4 blocks.

BASKET WITH PAPER-PIECED CRAZY-PATCH CENTER BLOCK

Refer to pages 42-44 for guidance. Make 4 blocks.

Quilt Top Construction

Press following the arrows.

1. Cut four short filler strips 1 ½" x 8 ½".
2. Cut two long sashing strips 1 ½" x 30 ½".
3. Arrange the blocks and strips as shown.
4. Sew the blocks and filler strips into rows and press. Sew the rows and sashing strips together. Press.

Inner Border

1. Cut two 1 ½" x 30 ½" strips for the top and bottom and two 1 ½" x 32 ½" strips for the sides.

2. Sew on the inner border (first the shorter top and bottom strips, then the longer side strips). Press.

Flying Geese Border

Refer to pages 23-24 and 25 for guidance.

1. Make 18 photocopies of the Flying Geese Border pattern (5 for the top, 5 for the bottom, and 4 for each side border). Cut out the paper patterns on the dashed lines. Tape the paper patterns together for each border, matching the lines. Be sure there is ¼" seam allowance on all sides. (Add the dashed line if necessary.) You will need 18 + 2 Flying Geese for the top, 18 + 2 for the bottom, and 16 for each side border.

2. Paper piece the side Flying Geese borders.

3. Attach the side borders. Press.

4. Paper piece the top and bottom Flying Geese border sections. Paper piece the Flying Geese border corner sections.

5. Refer to the illustration for the correct placement and attach a border corner section to the right end of the top border section.

6. Attach this border to the top edge of the quilt. Press.

7. Refer to the illustration for the correct placement and attach a border corner section to the left end of the bottom border section.

8. Attach this border to the bottom edge of the quilt. Press.

9. Carefully remove the paper.

Congratulations, I hope you had fun playing with these blocks! Now it's time to layer, baste, and quilt following the General Instructions beginning on page 8.

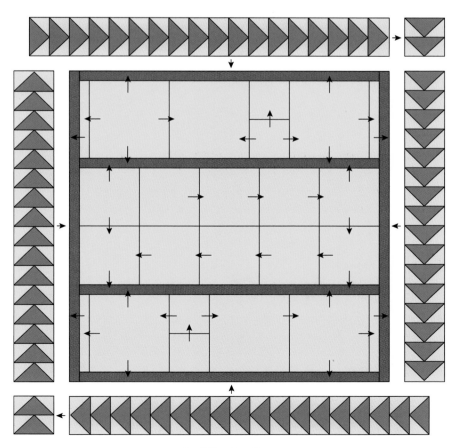

Quilt Construction

About the Author

Alex Anderson's love affair with quiltmaking began in 1978, when she completed her Grandmother's Flower Garden quilt as part of her work toward a degree in art at San Francisco State University. Over the years her focus has rested upon understanding fabric relationships, and an intense appreciation of traditional quilting surface design and star quilts.

Alex currently hosts Home and Garden Television's quilt show *Simply Quilts*. Her quilts have been shown in magazines, including several articles specifically about her works.

Alex lives in Northern California with her husband, two children, two cats, one dog, one fish, and the challenges of suburban life. Visit her website at alexandersonquilts.com.

For more information write for a free catalog:
C&T Publishing, Inc.
P.O. Box 1456
Lafayette, CA 94549
(800) 284-1114
e-mail: ctinfo@ctpub.com
website: www.ctpub.com

For quilting supplies:
Cotton Patch Mail Order
3405 Hall Lane, Dept. CTB
Lafayette, CA 94549
(800) 835-4418
(925) 283-7883
e-mail: quiltusa@yahoo.com
website: www.quiltusa.com

Please Note:
Fabrics used in the quilts shown may not be currently available since fabric manufacturers keep most fabrics in print for only a short time.

Other books by Alex Anderson:

   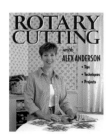